KYOTO TRAVEL GUIDE

BEYOND

A Comprehensive Handbook for Exploring the Best of

Japan's Cultural Capital

HARUTO KENJI

Haruto Kenji

TABLE OF CONTENT

Introduction

Welcome to Kyoto Travel Guide 2023 and Beyond, your indispensable companion to exploring the best of Japan's cultural capital. With its rich history, stunning architecture, and vibrant cultural scene, Kyoto is a must-visit destination for anyone looking to experience the essence of traditional Japan. This comprehensive guide will provide you with all the information you need to make the most of your trip to this enchanting city, whether you're a first-time visitor or a seasoned traveler.

Delve into the ancient history of Kyoto as we uncover the stories behind its iconic temples, shrines, and palaces. Learn about the unique customs and traditions that have been passed down through generations, and immerse yourself in the tranquil beauty of the city's zen gardens and bamboo forests.

Kyoto Travel Guide 2023 And Beyond

Discover Kyoto's diverse culinary landscape, from elegant kaiseki dining to the bustling Nishiki Market, where you can sample local delicacies and street food. We'll introduce you to the best places to eat, drink, and shop in the city, including hidden gems and off-the-beaten-path spots that only locals know about.

Explore the city's vibrant arts and crafts scene, with a focus on traditional techniques such as kimono weaving, pottery, and woodblock printing. Uncover the secrets of the geisha world, and learn about the city's thriving contemporary art scene.

In addition to covering all the must-see sights and attractions, this guide will provide you with practical information on transportation, accommodation, and safety, as well as insider tips and recommendations to help you plan the perfect itinerary.

Kyoto Travel Guide 2023 and Beyond is your one-stop resource for making your trip to Kyoto an unforgettable journey. So pack your bags, dust off your camera, and get ready to embark on an adventure that will leave you with memories to last a lifetime.

CHAPTER ONE

Getting To Know Kyoto

In this chapter, we will introduce you to the captivating city of Kyoto, providing you with essential information to help you get acquainted with its history, culture, and geography. We will also discuss the city's climate and the best times to visit, ensuring you have the most enjoyable experience possible.

History of Kyoto

Kyoto, a city steeped in history and tradition, served as Japan's capital and the emperor's residence from 794 to 1868. With more than a thousand years of history, Kyoto is home to an unparalleled collection of temples, shrines, and other architectural marvels that testify to the city's rich cultural heritage.

The founding of Kyoto, originally called Heian-kyo, marked the beginning of the Heian period (794-1185). During this time, the city was meticulously planned, with its grid-like layout inspired by the Chinese capital of Chang'an. As the center of Japanese politics and culture, Kyoto witnessed the flourishing of literature, art, and religion, including the emergence of Buddhism as a significant influence.

The Kamakura period (1185-1333) brought about the decline of imperial power, as the samurai class gained prominence. Despite the shift in political power, Kyoto

11

remained the cultural heart of Japan, with the city's elegant aristocratic culture persisting during this time.

In the Muromachi period (1336-1573), Kyoto witnessed the rise of the Ashikaga shogunate, a powerful military government. This era is characterized by the development of new forms of Japanese art, such as ink painting and the tea ceremony. It also saw the construction of famous Zen temples and gardens, which remain iconic landmarks of Kyoto today.

During the Azuchi-Momoyama period (1573-1603), warlords Oda Nobunaga and Toyotomi Hideyoshi contributed to the unification of Japan. Under their rule, Kyoto experienced a resurgence in culture and the arts, with the construction of grand castles and palaces.

The Edo period (1603-1868) marked a time of relative peace and stability under the Tokugawa shogunate. While the political center shifted to Edo (present-day Tokyo), Kyoto continued to thrive as a center for traditional arts and crafts. The city also became known for its geisha culture and tea ceremonies.

In 1868, the Meiji Restoration marked the end of the shogunate and the beginning of modern Japan. The emperor moved from Kyoto to Tokyo, and Kyoto lost its status as the capital. However, this change also spared the city from the extensive modernization that occurred in other Japanese cities during this period.

Today, Kyoto remains an essential destination for anyone seeking to experience Japan's cultural and historical wealth. The city boasts 17 UNESCO World Heritage sites, countless temples and shrines, and numerous traditional tea houses and geisha districts. Kyoto's enduring charm lies in its harmonious blend of ancient tradition and modernity, making it a must-visit destination for travelers from around the world.

Geography

Kyoto is located in the central part of Honshu, the main island of Japan, and is part of the Kansai region. It lies in a valley surrounded by mountains on three sides, with the Higashiyama range to the east, Kitayama range to the north, and Nishiyama range to the west. This geographical setting has played a significant role in shaping Kyoto's climate, history, and cultural identity.

Covering an area of approximately 827.8 square kilometers (319.6 square miles), Kyoto is characterized by its urban core and several surrounding suburban districts. The city stretches from north to south, with the Kamo River running through the heart of Kyoto, dividing the city into eastern and western halves.

Kyoto's natural setting has played a key role in its development as a cultural center. The mountains surrounding the city provided natural protection from potential invaders, as well as materials for the construction of temples and shrines. Additionally, the Kamo River and Lake Biwa, Japan's largest freshwater lake, located northeast of Kyoto, have been essential sources of water for the city's inhabitants.

The city's layout, with its well-organized grid pattern, has its origins in the Heian period (794-1185), when the city was modeled after the Chinese capital of Chang'an. This design facilitated the easy flow of people, goods, and ideas throughout Kyoto, contributing to its development as a thriving cultural center.

Kyoto's geography has also influenced its climate, which is characterized by four distinct seasons. The city experiences hot and humid summers, with temperatures often exceeding 30°C (86°F), while winters can be quite cold, with temperatures occasionally dropping below freezing. Spring and autumn offer milder, more comfortable weather, with cherry blossoms in spring and vibrant fall foliage in autumn, making these seasons popular times to visit the city.

People and Culture

Kyoto is a city deeply rooted in tradition and culture, which is reflected in the daily lives of its people. With a population of approximately 1.5 million, Kyoto is home to a diverse mix of people, including long-time residents, students, and a growing number of international residents.

The people of Kyoto are known for their warm hospitality, politeness, and strong sense of cultural preservation. They take great pride in maintaining the city's historical sites, and many locals still practice traditional arts and crafts, such as tea ceremony, kimono dressing, and calligraphy.

Kyoto is often considered the cultural heart of Japan, and it has played a pivotal role in the development of Japanese arts, crafts, and traditions. The city is home to numerous temples, shrines, and UNESCO World Heritage sites, which have helped to shape the cultural identity of Kyoto and its people. Residents of Kyoto have a deep appreciation for their city's history and cultural heritage, and this appreciation is evident in their daily lives, festivals, and celebrations.

Kyoto's rich cultural heritage also extends to its culinary scene, which is renowned for its delicate flavors and meticulous presentation. Traditional kaiseki ryori, a multi-course Japanese meal, is a highlight of the city's cuisine, as are matcha green tea and wagashi (Japanese sweets).

The people of Kyoto are known for their adherence to traditional customs and etiquette, which can be observed in their daily interactions and during special events and celebrations. For example, it is common to see residents wearing traditional kimonos during festivals and other important occasions. Additionally, the people of Kyoto value the concept of omotenashi, or Japanese-style hospitality, which emphasizes the importance of anticipating the needs of guests and providing a warm, welcoming experience.

In recent years, Kyoto has become more cosmopolitan, with an influx of foreign residents and tourists. This has led to a greater diversity in the city's culture and the emergence of new, innovative ideas and trends. Despite these changes, Kyoto remains a city deeply connected to its history and traditions, with its people dedicated to preserving the unique cultural heritage that makes Kyoto so special.

Climate

Kyoto's climate is characterized as humid subtropical, with four distinct seasons: spring, summer, autumn, and winter. Each season offers its own unique experiences, making Kyoto an attractive destination throughout the year.

Spring (March to May) is a favorite time to visit Kyoto, as the weather is mild and comfortable, with average temperatures ranging from 10°C to 20°C (50°F to 68°F). This is also the season when cherry blossoms (sakura) bloom, creating stunning landscapes across the city. The cherry blossom season usually peaks around late March to early April, attracting many visitors who come to enjoy the breathtaking sight of the delicate pink flowers.

Summer (June to August) in Kyoto can be hot and humid, with temperatures sometimes exceeding 30°C

(86°F). The rainy season, known as tsuyu, typically occurs in June and early July, bringing increased humidity and frequent rainfall. Despite the heat and humidity, summer is an exciting time to visit Kyoto, as numerous festivals and events take place, such as the famous Gion Matsuri in July.

Autumn (September to November) is another popular time to visit Kyoto, as the weather cools down and becomes more pleasant. Average temperatures range from 15°C to 25°C (59°F to 77°F). Autumn foliage, particularly the vibrant red and golden hues of maple leaves, is a significant draw for visitors during this season. The peak of the autumn colors usually occurs in mid-November, creating breathtaking scenes throughout the city's temples and gardens.

Winter (December to February) in Kyoto is generally cold but not severe, with average temperatures ranging from 1°C to 10°C (34°F to 50°F). Snowfall is relatively rare in Kyoto but can create enchanting views when it occurs, especially at the city's historic temples and shrines. Winter is also a great time to visit Kyoto's many onsen (hot springs) and enjoy traditional Japanese winter cuisine.

When planning a trip to Kyoto, it's essential to consider the climate and choose the season that best aligns with your interests and preferences. Each season offers its own charm and beauty, ensuring a memorable experience regardless of when you choose to visit.

Unique Attractions

Kyoto is known for its unique attractions that showcase the city's rich history, cultural heritage, and natural beauty. Some of the most notable attractions include:

Kinkaku-ji (Golden Pavilion)

Kinkaku-ji, also known as the Golden Pavilion, is a Zen Buddhist temple and one of Kyoto's most iconic attractions. It is officially named Rokuon-ji, but it is commonly referred to as Kinkaku-ji due to its unique appearance. The temple is situated in the northwest part of Kyoto, surrounded by a beautiful Japanese strolling garden and a pond called Kyoko-chi (Mirror Pond).

The Golden Pavilion was originally built in 1397 as a retirement villa for the shogun Ashikaga Yoshimitsu. After his death, the villa was converted into a Zen Buddhist temple, as per his wishes. The temple has been burned down and rebuilt several times throughout its history, with the current structure dating back to 1955.

Kinkaku-ji's most striking feature is its two upper floors, which are covered in gold leaf. The temple's design is a harmonious blend of different architectural styles, representing the shogun's aspirations for unity and peace. The first floor, known as the Chamber of Dharma Waters, is built in the shinden-zukuri style, which is typical of aristocratic residences from the Heian Period. The second floor, called the Tower of Sound Waves, is constructed in the buke-zukuri style, associated with samurai residences. The top floor, known as the Cupola of the Ultimate, features a Chinese-inspired Zen hall style, called zenshu-butsuden-zukuri.

The golden pavilion is topped with a bronze phoenix ornament, adding to the temple's sense of grandeur. The reflection of the pavilion shimmering on the pond creates a breathtaking scene, particularly during sunrise and sunset, making it a popular spot for photography.

Within the temple grounds, visitors can also find the Sekka-tei Teahouse, a small traditional teahouse where they can experience a Japanese tea ceremony. The garden surrounding Kinkaku-ji is a designated historic site and a place of scenic beauty, with carefully arranged trees, stones, and moss-covered grounds.

Kinkaku-ji is an essential stop for anyone visiting Kyoto, offering a glimpse into Japan's rich history, cultural heritage, and exquisite architectural traditions.

Fushimi Inari Taisha

Fushimi Inari Taisha is a famous Shinto shrine located in southern Kyoto, dedicated to Inari, the Shinto god of rice, agriculture, and business prosperity. Founded in 711 AD, it is the head shrine of more than 30,000 Inari shrines across Japan. Fushimi Inari Taisha is best known for its thousands of vermilion torii gates that create an incredible tunnel-like path up the forested Mount Inari.

The main entrance to the shrine is marked by the impressive Romon Gate, which was donated by the renowned samurai Toyotomi Hideyoshi in 1589. After passing through the gate, visitors will find the main hall (honden) where they can pay their respects and offer prayers for good fortune and success.

The most iconic feature of Fushimi Inari Taisha is the Senbon Torii, or "thousands of torii gates," that line the hiking trails leading up to the summit of Mount Inari. Each torii gate is donated by individuals or businesses, with the donor's name and date of the donation inscribed on the back of each gate. The vibrant vermilion color is believed to ward off evil spirits and is associated with the power of Inari.

The hike to the summit of Mount Inari takes around 2-3 hours, depending on your pace. Along the way, you will encounter numerous smaller shrines, stone fox statues, and scenic viewpoints overlooking the city of Kyoto. Foxes, or kitsune, are considered messengers of Inari and are often depicted with a key in their mouths, symbolizing the key to the rice granary.

Aside from the main shrine and the torii gates, Fushimi Inari Taisha also features a variety of teahouses and small restaurants offering local delicacies. Inari sushi, a type of sushi made with sweetened rice wrapped in deep-fried tofu, is a popular snack among visitors.

Fushimi Inari Taisha is an unmissable destination for anyone traveling to Kyoto. The striking torii gates, the serene atmosphere, and the rich cultural heritage make it a truly unique and unforgettable experience.

Arashiyama Bamboo Grove

Arashiyama Bamboo Grove, also known as Sagano Bamboo Forest, is a mesmerizing natural attraction in the Arashiyama district of Kyoto. Known for its towering bamboo stalks that stretch towards the sky, the grove creates a serene and otherworldly atmosphere that attracts visitors from all over the world. The rustling sound of the bamboo leaves swaying in the breeze is considered one of the "100 Soundscapes of Japan" by the Japanese Ministry of the Environment.

The Bamboo Grove is easily accessible from the Arashiyama train station and can be combined with a visit to other nearby attractions such as Tenryu-ji Temple, a UNESCO World Heritage site, and the scenic Togetsukyo Bridge, which spans the Katsura River.

Walking through the Bamboo Grove, you will find yourself surrounded by the lush greenery of the bamboo stalks, which create a natural canopy above you. The tall, slender bamboo creates an almost surreal ambience, providing a calming respite from the bustling city of Kyoto. The pathway through the grove is well-maintained and stretches for approximately 500 meters, making it a pleasant and easily accessible walk for visitors of all ages.

The Arashiyama Bamboo Grove is particularly stunning in the early morning or late afternoon when the sunlight filters through the bamboo stalks, casting enchanting shadows on the ground. The grove is also beautiful during the evening when the path is illuminated, creating a magical atmosphere.

For a unique experience, you can also take a traditional rickshaw ride through the bamboo forest. The knowledgeable rickshaw drivers often provide interesting insights into the history and culture of Arashiyama, making it a memorable and informative way to explore the area.

A visit to Arashiyama Bamboo Grove is a must for anyone traveling to Kyoto, as it offers a peaceful and enchanting experience that showcases the natural beauty and tranquility of Japan.

Kiyomizu-dera

Kiyomizu-dera, officially known as Otowa-san Kiyomizu-dera, is an iconic Buddhist temple in the Higashiyama district of Kyoto, Japan. Founded in 778, the temple is part of the Historic Monuments of Ancient Kyoto, a UNESCO World Heritage Site. Kiyomizu-dera is dedicated to the goddess of mercy, Kannon, and is one of the most celebrated temples in Japan, attracting millions of visitors annually.

The temple's name, Kiyomizu, translates to "pure water," which comes from the sacred Otowa Waterfall that flows within the temple grounds. The waterfall is believed to have healing properties, and visitors can drink the water using cups attached to long poles for health, longevity, and success.

One of the most remarkable features of Kiyomizu-dera is its main hall, which has a large wooden stage that juts out over the hillside, offering stunning panoramic views of Kyoto. The stage is supported by a complex lattice of wooden pillars and beams, constructed without the use of nails. The architectural prowess of this structure is a testament to the skills of ancient Japanese craftsmen.

Surrounding the main hall are various other halls, pagodas, and shrines, each with their own unique features and historical significance. The Jishu Shrine, located behind the main hall, is dedicated to the god of love and matchmaking. Visitors seeking love and a happy marriage often come to this shrine to pray and participate in rituals.

Kiyomizu-dera is particularly popular during the cherry blossom season in spring and the autumn foliage season. The vibrant colors of the cherry blossoms and the red and orange hues of the autumn leaves create a breathtaking backdrop for the temple, making it a favorite spot for photographers and nature lovers alike.

Visiting Kiyomizu-dera is a must for anyone traveling to Kyoto, as it offers a unique blend of history, architecture, and natural beauty, providing an unforgettable experience of Japan's rich cultural heritage.

Gion

Gion is Kyoto's most famous geisha district, located around Shijo Avenue between Yasaka Shrine in the east and the Kamo River in the west. Gion is an enchanting area filled with traditional wooden machiya merchant houses, teahouses (ochaya), and exclusive restaurants, providing a glimpse into the city's rich cultural past.

Historically, Gion developed as a result of the establishment of Yasaka Shrine and catered to the needs of travelers and visitors to the shrine. Over time, the area became one of the most prominent entertainment districts in Japan, with geisha, or geiko as they are called in Kyoto, entertaining guests with traditional music, dance, and conversation.

As you stroll through the atmospheric streets of Gion, you might be lucky enough to spot a geisha or a maiko (an apprentice geisha) on their way to or from an engagement at a teahouse. The sight of these elegant and mysterious figures, dressed in exquisite kimono and wearing traditional makeup, is an unforgettable experience.

One of the best places to spot geisha in Gion is Hanami-koji Street, a charming, cobblestone-paved street lined with traditional buildings and exclusive establishments.

Another popular area is the Shirakawa district, located along the Shirakawa Canal, which offers a picturesque setting with willow trees and old-style wooden buildings.

Gion is also home to several cultural landmarks, such as the Kennin-ji Temple, the oldest Zen temple in Kyoto, and the Yasaka Shrine, a popular destination for locals and tourists alike. Additionally, the district has numerous shops selling traditional Kyoto crafts, souvenirs, and local sweets.

If you want to immerse yourself in the geisha culture, you can attend a cultural show at Gion Corner, where you can enjoy performances of traditional Japanese arts, such as tea ceremonies, flower arrangement, and puppet theater.

Visiting Gion is an essential part of any trip to Kyoto, as it offers a rare opportunity to experience the city's history, culture, and traditional entertainment in an enchanting setting.

Nijo Castle

Nijo Castle, located in the heart of Kyoto, is a historic site that showcases the architectural splendor of Japan's feudal era. Built in 1603 as the residence for Tokugawa Ieyasu, the first shogun of the Edo Period (1603-1867), the castle complex is spread over 275,000 square meters and is surrounded by stone walls and moats. Nijo Castle was designated as a UNESCO World Heritage Site in

1994, along with several other historical monuments in Kyoto.

The castle complex consists of two main sections: the Ninomaru Palace and the Honmaru Palace. The Ninomaru Palace is the main attraction, featuring a series of elegant chambers with sliding doors adorned with beautiful paintings by the Kano school, one of the most famous schools of Japanese painting. The palace's interior is characterized by its "nightingale floors," which squeak when walked on – a security feature designed to alert residents to the presence of intruders.

The Honmaru Palace, located within the inner walls, was originally built in 1601 and later reconstructed in 1893 after being destroyed by a fire. This palace served as the shogun's residence and the site for important ceremonies. Although not always open to the public, visitors can still appreciate the beautiful gardens surrounding the palace and enjoy panoramic views of Kyoto from the castle's stone foundation.

In addition to the palaces, Nijo Castle boasts several beautiful gardens, including the Ninomaru Garden, a traditional Japanese landscape garden designed by the famed landscape architect and tea master Kobori Enshu. The garden features a large pond with three islands, stone bridges, and meticulously manicured pine trees.

Nijo Castle offers visitors a fascinating glimpse into the opulence and grandeur of Japan's feudal era. As you explore the castle grounds, you'll gain insight into the lives of the shoguns who ruled Japan for over 260 years and the exquisite art and craftsmanship that characterized the period. Don't miss the opportunity to visit this important historical site during your time in Kyoto.

Philosopher's Path

The Philosopher's Path, or Tetsugaku-no-michi, is a picturesque and tranquil walking route in Kyoto, stretching approximately 2 kilometers along a stone-paved path. It follows a canal lined with hundreds of cherry trees and connects the Ginkaku-ji (Silver Pavilion) in the north to the Nanzen-ji temple in the south. Named after the famous Japanese philosopher Nishida Kitaro, who was said to have meditated along this path during his daily walks, the Philosopher's Path is a popular destination for both tourists and locals.

The path is particularly stunning during cherry blossom season (usually in late March to early April) when the cherry trees form a beautiful tunnel of blossoms over the path. Fall foliage season, typically in late November, is another great time to visit, as the path becomes enveloped in vibrant hues of red, orange, and yellow.

As you stroll along the Philosopher's Path, you'll come across several temples, shrines, and other points of interest. Some of the notable attractions include:

- Ginkaku-ji (Silver Pavilion): This Zen temple, initially intended to be covered in silver, features a beautiful sand garden and a moss garden with a circular walking route.
- Honen-in: A serene temple with a thatched gate, tranquil gardens, and a pond that reflects the surrounding maple and cherry trees.

- Eikan-do Zenrin-ji: A temple famous for its stunning fall foliage and beautiful pagoda, which offers panoramic views of Kyoto.
- Nanzen-ji: An important Zen temple with a massive entrance gate, beautiful rock gardens, and an aqueduct that runs through the temple grounds.

In addition to these attractions, there are numerous smaller temples, shrines, and cafes along the path, offering visitors plenty of opportunities to relax, explore, and soak in the serene atmosphere. The Philosopher's Path is an ideal destination for a leisurely walk, allowing you to experience the beauty and tranquility that Kyoto is famous for.

Ryoan-ji

Ryoan-ji is a Zen Buddhist temple located in the northwest of Kyoto, Japan, and is renowned for its unique and exquisite rock garden. The temple, whose name translates to "The Temple of the Dragon at Peace," is a UNESCO World Heritage site and belongs to the Myoshin-ji school of the Rinzai sect of Zen

Buddhism. Ryoan-ji was originally built in 1450 and has seen several reconstructions due to fires and other damages.

The temple's most famous feature is its karesansui (dry landscape) rock garden, which is a masterpiece of Japanese Zen garden design. The rectangular garden measures 30 meters from east to west and 10 meters from north to south. It is enclosed by clay walls and features 15 carefully arranged rocks of varying sizes, surrounded by white gravel that is meticulously raked to create a sense of tranquility and stillness.

One fascinating aspect of Ryoan-ji's rock garden is that, from any vantage point, only 14 rocks are visible at once. It is said that to see the 15th rock, one must attain spiritual enlightenment. The garden's minimalist design and its arrangement of rocks are open to various interpretations, with the most common one being that they represent islands in a sea or peaks of mountains rising above the clouds.

In addition to the rock garden, Ryoan-ji also boasts a beautiful pond garden called Kyoyochi, which dates back to the 12th century. The pond is surrounded by lush greenery and features a few small islands, making it an ideal spot for quiet contemplation.

Visiting Ryoan-ji offers a unique and serene experience, allowing you to immerse yourself in the tranquil atmosphere of the temple grounds and appreciate the elegance and simplicity of Japanese Zen garden design. The temple is a must-visit destination for anyone traveling to Kyoto and seeking to experience the city's rich cultural and spiritual heritage.

Kyoto International Manga Museum

The Kyoto International Manga Museum is a must-visit destination for manga enthusiasts and anyone interested in Japanese pop culture. Located in the former Tatsuike Elementary School in Nakagyo Ward,

Kyoto, the museum opened its doors in 2006 as a joint project between Kyoto City and Kyoto Seika University. The museum's primary purpose is to preserve, study, and showcase manga culture from Japan and around the world.

Boasting a vast collection of over 300,000 manga, the Kyoto International Manga Museum is one of the largest establishments of its kind. The collection includes both contemporary and historical manga, as well as international comics and graphic novels. The museum's Wall of Manga is a particularly impressive feature, displaying tens of thousands of manga volumes lining the shelves along the museum's corridors. Visitors are free to browse and read any of the manga at their leisure, with many choosing to sit in the museum's courtyard or indoor reading spaces while enjoying their selected works.

In addition to the extensive manga collection, the museum also hosts various exhibitions, workshops, and events. These activities aim to promote manga culture and engage visitors with the art form, often featuring manga artists, animators, and other industry professionals. There are also exhibits dedicated to the history and development of manga, offering a fascinating insight into its origins and evolution over the years.

The Kyoto International Manga Museum caters to an international audience, with a section dedicated to foreign-language manga and comics. There is also a museum shop that offers a variety of manga-related merchandise, including books, postcards, and souvenirs.

Whether you are a manga aficionado or new to the world of Japanese comics, the Kyoto International Manga Museum provides an entertaining and educational experience that immerses visitors in the rich world of manga culture.

These are just a few of the many unique attractions that make Kyoto a captivating destination for visitors who want to experience the best of Japan's cultural capital.

This chapter provides an overview of Kyoto's history, culture, and geography. You'll learn about the city's four main districts, as well as its many neighborhoods and attractions. You'll also get tips on the

How to navigate the city's transportation system

Navigating Kyoto's transportation system is fairly easy, as it is well-organized and efficient. The city offers a variety of public transportation options, including trains, buses, and taxis, making it convenient for travelers to explore all that Kyoto has to offer.

Trains: Trains are one of the most popular modes of transportation in Kyoto. The city is serviced by two primary train operators: JR West (Japan Railways) and the private companies Keihan, Hankyu, and Kintetsu. The main train stations in Kyoto are Kyoto Station, which is the city's central transportation hub, and Kawaramachi Station, located in the heart of downtown.

JR West: The JR lines are useful for reaching popular attractions such as Arashiyama, Fushimi Inari Taisha, and Nijo Castle. The JR Sagano Line connects Kyoto Station to Arashiyama, while the JR Nara Line connects Kyoto Station to Fushimi Inari Taisha and the JR Kyoto Line links the city to Osaka and Nara.

Keihan, Hankyu, and Kintetsu: These private railway companies operate lines that connect Kyoto to nearby cities like Osaka, Nara, and Uji. The Keihan Main Line is useful for reaching the Gion district and Kiyomizu-dera Temple, while the Hankyu Kyoto Line connects Kyoto to Osaka's Umeda Station.

Buses: Kyoto's bus network is extensive and serves most tourist destinations within the city. The buses are operated by Kyoto City Bus and Kyoto Bus. The flat-rate buses, identified by their green or yellow color, are particularly convenient for tourists, as they cover the central area of Kyoto for a fixed fare. Bus stops usually display route maps and timetables in English, making it easy for foreign visitors to navigate the system.

Taxis: Taxis are a convenient but more expensive option for getting around Kyoto. They can be hailed on the street or found at taxi stands near major train stations and tourist attractions. Most taxis accept cash and some also accept credit cards. Keep in mind that taxis in Kyoto are metered, and fares increase at night.

Bicycles: Kyoto is a bicycle-friendly city, with many rental shops offering bikes for hourly or daily rates. Exploring the city by bike allows for greater flexibility and access to areas that may not be as easily reachable by public transportation.

When planning your trip around Kyoto, consider purchasing a transportation pass, such as the Kyoto City Bus One-Day Pass or the Kansai Thru Pass, which can save you money on fares and provide unlimited travel on certain transportation services. Don't forget to pick up a transportation map, available at major train stations, bus stops, and tourist information centers, to help you navigate Kyoto's public transportation system with ease.

CHAPTER TWO

Exploring Kyoto's Temples and Shrines

Kyoto is renowned for its historic temples and shrines, which are an integral part of the city's rich cultural heritage. With over 2,000 temples and shrines scattered throughout the city, Kyoto offers a unique opportunity for visitors to immerse themselves in the beauty and serenity of these sacred places. In this chapter, we will discuss some of the most iconic and must-visit temples and shrines in Kyoto, as well as provide helpful tips for making the most of your temple-hopping experience.

Kinkaku-ji (Golden Pavilion)

Kinkaku-ji, also known as the Golden Pavilion, is a magnificent Zen Buddhist temple located in the northern part of Kyoto, Japan. It is officially known as Rokuon-ji, which translates to "Deer Garden Temple." Kinkaku-ji is one of the most popular and iconic tourist attractions in Kyoto, drawing visitors from all over the world.

History

The history of Kinkaku-ji dates back to the 14th century when it was built as a retirement villa for Shogun Ashikaga Yoshimitsu. Following his death in 1408, the villa was converted into a Zen temple in accordance with his wishes. The temple has been destroyed and rebuilt several times over the centuries, with the most recent reconstruction taking place in 1955 after a young monk set fire to the pavilion.

Architecture

Kinkaku-ji's main attraction is the golden pavilion itself, a three-story building covered in gold leaf. Each story showcases a different architectural style. The first floor, called the Chamber of Dharma Waters, is built in the Shinden style, which was popular during the Heian period. The second floor, called the Tower of Sound Waves, features the Bukke style commonly seen in samurai residences. The third floor, known as the Cupola of the Ultimate, is designed in the Zen-influenced Chinese style and is topped with a golden phoenix.

Gardens and Grounds

The temple grounds are a fine example of Muromachi period garden design. The Golden Pavilion is situated next to a large pond called Kyoko-chi (Mirror Pond), which reflects the pavilion beautifully. The pond is home to several islands and stones, each with its own symbolic meaning. The meticulously maintained gardens surrounding the pavilion are a stunning example of Japanese landscape design and feature various trees, mosses, and carefully placed stones.

Visiting Kinkaku-ji

Kinkaku-ji is open daily from 900 AM to 500 PM, and there is a small entrance fee for visitors. Upon entering the temple grounds, visitors follow a designated path that leads around the pond, offering multiple vantage points to admire and photograph the Golden Pavilion. The path also takes you through the temple gardens, past a small teahouse, and finally to a souvenir shop and the exit.

Keep in mind that visitors are not allowed to enter the pavilion itself, but can appreciate its stunning beauty from the outside. Additionally, it's important to be respectful and follow the guidelines for proper behavior when visiting the temple, as it is a sacred place for many Buddhists.

Fushimi Inari Taisha

Fushimi Inari Taisha is an important Shinto shrine located in Kyoto, Japan. It is famous for its thousands of vermilion torii gates, which create a striking visual experience for visitors. The shrine is dedicated to Inari, the Shinto god of rice, prosperity, and business, and is the head shrine for over 30,000 Inari shrines across Japan.

History

Fushimi Inari Taisha dates back to 711 AD, making it one of the oldest and most significant shrines in Kyoto. The shrine's popularity grew during the Edo period (1603-1868) when merchants and manufacturers came to offer prayers for success in business and a good harvest. The tradition continues to this day, with businesses donating torii gates as a symbol of gratitude for their prosperity.

Torii Gates

The most iconic feature of Fushimi Inari Taisha is the seemingly endless rows of vermilion torii gates that cover the hiking trails leading up to the sacred Mount Inari. Each gate is donated by individuals or businesses seeking good fortune, and the donor's name and date of the donation are inscribed on the back of each gate. There are estimated to be around 10,000 torii gates at Fushimi Inari Taisha.

Hiking Trails

The shrine is nestled at the base of Mount Inari, which stands at 233 meters (764 feet) high. The main trail leading up the mountain takes about 2-3 hours to complete, depending on your pace. Along the way, you'll encounter numerous smaller shrines, stone fox statues, teahouses, and beautiful views of Kyoto. The foxes, or kitsune, are considered messengers of Inari and are often depicted holding a key in their mouths, symbolizing the key to the rice granaries.

Visiting Fushimi Inari Taisha

Fushimi Inari Taisha is open 24 hours a day and is free to enter. The best time to visit is early in the morning or late afternoon to avoid crowds. The shrine can be easily accessed from Kyoto Station via the JR Nara Line, with the journey taking only about 5 minutes to Inari Station.

As Fushimi Inari Taisha is a sacred site, it is important to be respectful and follow proper etiquette when visiting. This includes dressing modestly, keeping noise levels down, and not littering or disturbing the wildlife.

Kiyomizu-dera

Kiyomizu-dera, officially known as Otowa-san Kiyomizu-dera, is an iconic Buddhist temple in Kyoto, Japan. Founded in 778 AD, it is part of the Historic Monuments of Ancient Kyoto UNESCO World Heritage site. Kiyomizu-dera is famous for its wooden stage that offers breathtaking views of Kyoto and its surrounding hills. The temple is dedicated to Kannon, the goddess of mercy and compassion.

Architecture

The main hall of Kiyomizu-dera is an architectural marvel, with its massive wooden stage (Kiyomizu Stage) supported by 139 pillars, built without using a single nail. The stage was constructed using traditional Japanese techniques and offers a panoramic view of Kyoto. The main hall houses the temple's primary object of worship, a small wooden statue of Kannon, which is rarely displayed to the public.

Otowa Waterfall

Another significant feature of Kiyomizu-dera is the Otowa Waterfall, which flows from the hills above the temple. The waterfall is divided into three streams, each with a specific blessing longevity, success in studies, and a fortunate love life. Visitors can use cups attached to long poles to drink from the streams and receive the blessings. However, it is considered greedy to drink from all three, so choose wisely.

Jishu Shrine

Located within the temple grounds, Jishu Shrine is dedicated to the god of love and matchmaking, Okuninushi-no-Mikoto. The shrine features two love stones placed 18 meters apart. It is said that if one can walk from one stone to the other with their eyes closed, they will find true love. Visitors often attempt this challenge, with friends guiding them to ensure they reach the second stone successfully.

Visiting Kiyomizu-dera

Kiyomizu-dera is open daily from 600 am to 600 pm, with extended hours during special events and light-up periods. The temple requires an entrance fee, which varies depending on the time of year and whether the inner sanctum is open. To access Kiyomizu-dera, you can take a bus from Kyoto Station or walk from Kiyomizu-Gojo Station along the Keihan Railway Line. The walk from the station takes about 20 minutes and leads you through the picturesque Higashiyama District, where you can enjoy traditional shops and cafes along the way.

Ginkaku-ji (Silver Pavilion)

Ginkaku-ji, or the Silver Pavilion, is a stunning Zen temple located in Kyoto's Higashiyama district. Officially known as Jisho-ji, the temple was established in 1482 by Ashikaga Yoshimasa, the eighth shogun of the Ashikaga shogunate, as a retirement villa. Ginkaku-ji was later converted into a Zen temple after Yoshimasa's death. Although the temple was initially intended to be covered in silver, this plan was never realized, and the name "Silver Pavilion" remains a nickname.

Architecture and Gardens

Ginkaku-ji is known for its remarkable architecture, blending traditional Japanese and Chinese styles. The two-story Kannon Hall is the temple's main building, which houses a statue of Kannon, the goddess of mercy. The first floor, known as the Shinkuden, is designed in the Shoin style, while the second floor, called the Cho-on-do, follows the Chinese Zen Hall style.

The temple grounds feature a beautiful moss garden and a unique dry sand garden called the "Sea of Silver Sand." The sand garden has a large sand cone named "Moon Viewing Platform," which is said to symbolize Mount Fuji. The temple's gardens are meticulously maintained and offer serene walking paths that pass by ponds, bridges, and carefully arranged stones.

The Philosopher's Path

Ginkaku-ji is also the starting point of the Philosopher's Path (Tetsugaku-no-Michi), a two-kilometer-long stone path that follows a canal connecting Ginkaku-ji with Nanzen-ji Temple. This path was named after Nishida Kitaro, a famous Japanese philosopher, who used to walk this route for daily meditation. The Philosopher's Path is particularly popular during the cherry blossom season and offers a peaceful and scenic walk through the residential areas of Kyoto.

Visiting Ginkaku-ji

Ginkaku-ji is open daily from 830 am to 500 pm, with an entrance fee required for visitors. To access Ginkaku-ji, you can take the city bus number 5, 17, or 100 from Kyoto Station, or you can walk from the Demachiyanagi Station on the Keihan Railway Line, which takes about 25 minutes. The temple is a popular destination, so it's best to arrive early to avoid crowds.

Ryoan-ji

Ryoan-ji, located in the northwest of Kyoto, is a famous Zen temple that belongs to the Myoshinji school of the Rinzai sect. Founded in 1450 by Hosokawa Katsumoto, a prominent military leader during the Muromachi period, Ryoan-ji is particularly renowned for its mysterious and enigmatic rock garden, which is considered one of the finest examples of karesansui (dry landscape) design in Japan.

The Rock Garden

The main attraction at Ryoan-ji is its rock garden, which measures 30 meters from east to west and 10 meters from north to south. The garden consists of 15 carefully placed rocks of varying sizes, surrounded by white gravel. The rocks are arranged in such a way that visitors can only see 14 of them at any one time from any angle. It is believed that only when one attains spiritual enlightenment can they perceive the 15th rock. The designer of the garden remains unknown, and the meaning behind the rock arrangement is still a subject of debate, adding to its allure and mystique.

Surrounding Features

Besides the rock garden, Ryoan-ji also features a beautiful pond garden called Kyoyochi Pond, which dates back to the 12th century. The pond is surrounded by lush greenery, and visitors can enjoy a peaceful walk around it while admiring the seasonal changes in flora.

The temple grounds also include the main hall (Hojo), the Kuri building, and the teahouse known as Seigen'in. The Hojo, which was reconstructed in 1800 after a fire, displays traditional fusuma (sliding door) paintings and tatami mat flooring. The Kuri building functions as the temple's living quarters, while Seigen'in serves as a space for tea ceremonies and relaxation.

Visiting Ryoan-ji

Ryoan-ji is open daily from 800 am to 500 pm (March to November) and 830 am to 430 pm (December to February). There is an entrance fee for visitors. To reach Ryoan-ji, take the city bus number 50 or 59 from Kyoto Station, or alternatively, take the Keifuku Kitano Line to Ryoanji Station and walk for about 10 minutes. The temple can be quite crowded during peak seasons, so it is recommended to visit early in the morning for a quieter experience.

Nijo Castle

Nijo Castle, located in the heart of Kyoto, is a stunning example of early Edo-period architecture and a UNESCO World Heritage site. Built in 1603 by Tokugawa Ieyasu, the first shogun of the Edo period, Nijo Castle served as the Kyoto residence for the Tokugawa shogunate and as a symbol of the shogun's power and authority over the Imperial Court. The castle covers an area of approximately 275,000 square meters and is surrounded by stone walls and a wide moat.

Main Features:

- Ninomaru Palace: The main attraction within Nijo Castle is the Ninomaru Palace, a beautifully preserved wooden structure consisting of multiple buildings connected by corridors with 'nightingale floors' — floors that squeak when walked upon, serving as a security measure against intruders. The palace boasts elegantly decorated sliding doors, intricate wood carvings, and stunning wall paintings featuring scenes of nature and animals. The various rooms within the palace were used for meetings, receptions, and as living quarters for the shogun.

- Ninomaru Garden: Adjacent to the Ninomaru Palace, the Ninomaru Garden is a traditional Japanese landscape garden designed by the famed landscape architect and tea master, Kobori Enshu. The garden features a large pond with three islands, meandering pathways, meticulously pruned pine trees, and carefully placed stones, creating a serene and picturesque environment.

- Honmaru Palace and Garden: The Honmaru Palace was originally the residence of Emperor Komei before the Imperial Court was moved to Tokyo. The palace buildings were destroyed by fire, and the existing structure was relocated from the Imperial Palace grounds in 1893. The Honmaru Garden, although less refined than the Ninomaru Garden, still offers a pleasant, tranquil atmosphere.
- Castle walls and gates: Nijo Castle's massive stone walls and gates provide an impressive sight. The Karamon Gate, with its elaborate carvings and gold leaf decorations, is particularly noteworthy.

Visiting Nijo Castle: Nijo Castle is open to the public daily from 8:45 am to 5:00 pm (last entry at 4:00 pm) but is closed on Tuesdays in January, July, August, and

December, as well as on December 26 and January 4. There is an entrance fee for visitors.

To reach Nijo Castle, take the Karasuma subway line to Nijojo-mae Station, which is directly in front of the castle. Alternatively, you can take the city bus numbers 9, 50, or 101 from Kyoto Station to Nijojo-mae bus stop.

When visiting Nijo Castle, be prepared to remove your shoes before entering the palace buildings, and photography is not allowed inside the Ninomaru Palace.

When visiting Kyoto's temples and shrines, it's essential to be respectful of the customs and etiquette observed at these sacred places. Dress modestly, speak quietly, and follow any posted rules or guidelines. Many temples and shrines also charge a small entrance fee, which helps with the upkeep and preservation of these historic sites.

Plan your visits to temples and shrines around the opening hours, as some close earlier in the evening or have specific days when they are not open to the public. It's also a good idea to prioritize the temples and shrines you want to see, as it's not feasible to visit every single one during a short stay in Kyoto. Finally, consider visiting during off-peak hours or seasons to avoid crowds and enjoy a more serene experience.

How to avoid crowds and make the most of your visit

When visiting popular attractions like Kyoto's temples and shrines, avoiding crowds can greatly enhance your experience. Here are some tips on how to make the most of your visit while steering clear of the masses:

- Visit during the off-peak season: The peak seasons for tourism in Kyoto are spring (March to May) and autumn (October to November) when the cherry blossoms and fall foliage are at their peak, respectively. By visiting during the off-peak months (June, July, and September), you can avoid the largest crowds and still enjoy pleasant weather.

- Go early or late in the day: Many temples and shrines open early in the morning, and visiting at this time allows you to beat the majority of tourists. Alternatively, you can visit the attractions later in the afternoon, when most of the tour groups have moved on to other sites.

- Choose less-popular attractions: While it's hard to skip Kyoto's most famous temples and shrines, there are plenty of lesser-known yet equally impressive sites that are less crowded. By including some of these lesser-visited sites in your itinerary, you can enjoy a more peaceful experience.

- Visit on weekdays: Weekends and national holidays are generally busier, so plan your visit to popular attractions during the weekdays when the crowds are smaller.

- Purchase tickets in advance: Some popular sites offer advance ticket sales online, allowing you to skip the ticket lines and save time.

- Use a private guide: Hiring a private guide can help you navigate the city more efficiently and avoid the busiest times and places. They can also provide valuable insights and help tailor your itinerary to your interests.

- Be mindful of school holidays: Japanese school holidays can be particularly busy at popular tourist sites, so try to plan your visit around these times if possible.

- Stay in accommodations close to the attractions: Choosing accommodations near the attractions you want to visit can help you avoid the crowds by allowing you to visit the sites before the majority of tourists arrive.

By following these tips, you can make the most of your time in Kyoto and enjoy a more relaxed and fulfilling visit to its beautiful temples and shrines.

CHAPTER THREE

Discovering Kyoto's Gardens and Parks

In this chapter, we will explore the serene and beautiful gardens and parks that Kyoto has to offer. These tranquil spaces provide a perfect escape from the bustling city life and allow visitors to immerse themselves in the natural beauty and traditional Japanese landscaping techniques.

Arashiyama Bamboo Grove

Arashiyama Bamboo Grove is a magical and ethereal forest located in the western outskirts of Kyoto, Japan. Known for its towering bamboo stalks that seem to touch the sky, the grove has become an iconic and must-see destination for travelers to Kyoto.

The bamboo grove covers a vast area and features a walking path that takes visitors on a mesmerizing journey through the densely packed, towering green stalks. The path stretches approximately 500 meters, and the sunlight filtering through the bamboo creates a serene and otherworldly atmosphere that visitors will not soon forget.

Arashiyama Bamboo Grove is easily accessible by train from central Kyoto. Once you arrive at the Arashiyama station, it's a 10-15 minute walk to the entrance of the bamboo grove. The grove is open 24 hours a day, and there is no admission fee, making it a popular spot for tourists and locals alike.

While exploring the bamboo grove, make sure to also visit the nearby Tenryu-ji Temple, a UNESCO World Heritage Site known for its stunning gardens. The temple grounds also provide access to the bamboo grove, and the combination of the temple and the grove makes for a perfect half-day excursion.

The area surrounding the bamboo grove is filled with charming shops, restaurants, and teahouses, making it an ideal spot to enjoy a leisurely meal or tea break. Additionally, you can rent a bicycle to explore the picturesque Arashiyama area further or take a scenic boat ride on the Hozu River.

To avoid the crowds and fully experience the tranquility of Arashiyama Bamboo Grove, it's best to visit early in the morning or late in the afternoon. The magical atmosphere and calming sway of the bamboo stalks are sure to leave you in awe, making your visit to the Arashiyama Bamboo Grove an unforgettable experience.

Maruyama Park

Maruyama Park is a picturesque public park located in the Higashiyama District of Kyoto, Japan. Known for its beauty and tranquility, the park offers a serene escape from the city's bustling streets. With its beautiful landscape, traditional Japanese gardens, and a large pond at its center, Maruyama Park is a popular spot for locals and tourists alike.

One of the park's main attractions is its weeping cherry tree, or shidarezakura, which is illuminated at night during the cherry blossom season, typically between late March and early April. The park becomes a favorite hanami (cherry blossom viewing) spot, drawing large crowds who come to enjoy the stunning blossoms while picnicking under the trees.

Besides the cherry blossoms, Maruyama Park is home to several temples and shrines, including the famous Yasaka Shrine, Chion-in Temple, and Shoren-in Temple. These historic sites offer visitors the opportunity to experience traditional Japanese architecture and learn about the country's rich cultural heritage.

The park also features several teahouses and restaurants where visitors can enjoy a meal or a cup of tea while taking in the scenic beauty of the gardens. Some of the teahouses even offer outdoor seating, allowing guests to fully immerse themselves in the park's serene atmosphere.

Maruyama Park is easily accessible by public transportation. From Kyoto Station, take a city bus or subway to Gion, and then it's just a short walk to the park. The park is open year-round, and there is no admission fee.

Visiting Maruyama Park is a relaxing and enjoyable way to spend a day in Kyoto. Its picturesque gardens, historic temples and shrines, and beautiful cherry blossoms make it a must-see destination for anyone looking to experience the best of Kyoto's natural beauty and cultural heritage.

Philosopher's Path

The Philosopher's Path, or Tetsugaku-no-michi, is a scenic pedestrian walkway in Kyoto, Japan, that follows a tree-lined canal between Ginkaku-ji (Silver Pavilion) and Nanzen-ji Temple. Stretching approximately 2 kilometers (1.2 miles), the path gets its name from the influential Japanese philosopher, Nishida Kitaro, who was known to meditate and contemplate while walking this route on his daily commute to Kyoto University.

The Philosopher's Path is famous for its tranquil atmosphere and beautiful surroundings. The path is lined with cherry blossom trees, which bloom spectacularly during the spring season, attracting many visitors for hanami (cherry blossom viewing). The path is also surrounded by lush greenery, making it a delightful place to stroll and enjoy nature throughout the year.

Along the Philosopher's Path, you'll find numerous temples, shrines, and cultural sites to explore. Some notable attractions include Honen-in Temple, Otoyo Shrine, and Eikan-do Zenrin-ji Temple. These sites offer visitors a glimpse into Japan's rich spiritual and cultural heritage.

There are also several small shops, galleries, and cafes dotted along the path, where you can stop for refreshments or to purchase local crafts and souvenirs. Many of these establishments are housed in traditional

Japanese buildings, adding to the overall charm and ambiance of the area.

The Philosopher's Path is easily accessible by public transportation. From Kyoto Station, take the city bus or subway to Ginkaku-ji or Nanzen-ji, and then start your walk from either end of the path. The path itself is free to access, but some temples along the way may require an entrance fee.

A walk along the Philosopher's Path is a delightful way to spend a few hours in Kyoto, immersing yourself in the city's natural beauty and rich cultural heritage. It offers a serene escape from the hustle and bustle of the city and a chance to reflect on the beauty of life, just as Nishida Kitaro did many years ago.

Kyoto Botanical Garden

The Kyoto Botanical Garden, or Kyoto Shokubutsu-en, is a sprawling, lush green oasis located in the northern part of Kyoto, Japan. Covering an area of approximately 240,000 square meters (59 acres), it is the oldest and largest public botanical garden in the country, having been established in 1924. The garden is situated along the Kamogawa River and is easily accessible by public transportation, just a short walk from Kitayama Station on the Karasuma subway line.

Kyoto Botanical Garden is home to over 12,000 plant species, including both native Japanese flora and exotic plants from around the world. The garden is organized into various sections, such as the Cherry Blossom Garden, the Bonsai Garden, the European-style Parterre Garden, the Bamboo Garden, the Fern Garden, and the Conservatory, among others. Each section offers a unique and breathtaking display of botanical beauty, providing visitors with a rich and diverse experience.

The garden's impressive conservatory, which covers an area of 4,612 square meters (49,635 square feet), houses a vast collection of tropical and subtropical plants, including orchids, carnivorous plants, and various types of cacti. The conservatory is divided into different climate zones, allowing visitors to experience the incredible diversity of plant life found around the world.

Throughout the year, Kyoto Botanical Garden hosts various seasonal events and flower exhibitions, showcasing the beauty of the plants in bloom during different times of the year. The garden is particularly famous for its spectacular cherry blossoms in spring and vibrant autumn foliage, attracting numerous visitors during these seasons.

In addition to the stunning plant displays, the garden offers a variety of facilities, such as a visitor center, a restaurant, and a plant shop where you can purchase plants, gardening tools, and souvenirs. There are also several walking paths and benches throughout the garden, inviting visitors to relax and enjoy the serene, natural environment.

Kyoto Botanical Garden is a must-visit destination for nature lovers and plant enthusiasts visiting the city. The garden offers a tranquil escape from the bustling city streets and a chance to immerse yourself in the incredible world of plants.

Katsura Imperial Villa

The Katsura Imperial Villa, or Katsura Rikyu, is a stunning example of traditional Japanese architecture and garden design, located in the western suburbs of Kyoto. Built in the early Edo period (around the 17th century) by the ruling Hachijo-no-Miya family, the villa is regarded as one of the finest examples of Japanese aesthetics and craftsmanship.

The Katsura Imperial Villa complex consists of several beautifully designed wooden buildings, including the Old Shoin, the Middle Shoin, the New Palace, and various tea houses. These structures showcase the elegance and simplicity of Japanese architecture, featuring tatami mat floors, sliding paper doors, and traditional wooden joinery. The buildings are strategically positioned to provide stunning views of the surrounding landscape, blending harmoniously with nature.

The villa is perhaps best known for its expansive and meticulously maintained stroll garden, which covers an area of approximately 70,000 square meters (17 acres). The garden is designed in a circuit style, allowing visitors to walk along the meandering pathways and enjoy the ever-changing scenery. It features a large pond, carefully placed stone lanterns, charming wooden bridges, and an array of carefully pruned trees and shrubs. The garden is particularly famous for its seasonal beauty, with cherry blossoms in spring, vibrant greenery in summer, colorful foliage in autumn, and the serene atmosphere during winter.

Visiting the Katsura Imperial Villa requires advance reservation through the Imperial Household Agency, as the villa remains under the management of the Imperial Family. Tours are conducted in Japanese, but English audio guides are available to help visitors understand the historical and architectural significance of the site.

The Katsura Imperial Villa is a must-see attraction for those interested in traditional Japanese architecture, garden design, and the country's rich cultural history. A visit to this tranquil and elegant site offers a unique opportunity to experience the refined beauty and timeless charm of Japan's imperial past.

Shosei-en Garden

Shosei-en Garden, also known as Kikoku-tei, is a tranquil and picturesque Japanese garden located in the heart of Kyoto. It is associated with the Higashi Honganji Temple, one of the largest and most prominent temples in the city. This serene oasis was first established in the 17th century and was later redesigned in the 19th century after a series of fires.

Shosei-en Garden is designed in the kaiyu-shiki style, a traditional Japanese landscaping technique that features a central pond surrounded by carefully manicured trees, shrubs, and flowering plants. Visitors can stroll along the winding paths that encircle the pond, taking in the natural beauty and enjoying the ever-changing scenery.

The garden is home to several charming wooden structures, including a tea house, a guest house, and a traditional-style bridge. These buildings are excellent examples of classic Japanese architecture, characterized by their wooden frames, tatami mat floors, and sliding paper doors.

Shosei-en Garden is particularly famous for its seasonal beauty. In spring, the garden is adorned with delicate cherry blossoms, while the vibrant colors of maple trees take center stage in autumn. The lush greenery of summer and the quiet serenity of winter offer their own unique charms as well.

To reach Shosei-en Garden, it's just a short walk from Kyoto Station, making it easily accessible for visitors. The garden is open year-round and requires a small admission fee. Shosei-en Garden provides a peaceful and picturesque retreat from the bustling city, offering visitors a chance to experience the refined elegance of traditional Japanese garden design and immerse themselves in the timeless beauty of nature.

Murin-an Garden

Murin-an Garden is a hidden gem in Kyoto, a Japanese-style garden designed by famed landscape architect Ogawa Jihei VII between 1894 and 1898. It is a designated Place of Scenic Beauty in Japan and is known for its harmonious blend of natural and man-made elements. Located in the Sakyo Ward of Kyoto, the garden was originally the villa of Aritomo Yamagata, a prominent statesman and military leader during the Meiji Period.

The garden's design follows the concept of a "strolling garden," with a central pond and winding paths that take visitors on a journey through the beautifully landscaped grounds. One of the defining features of Murin-an Garden is its use of water, which is sourced from Lake Biwa through a small canal. The water flows through the garden, feeding the pond and several streams, creating an atmosphere of serenity and tranquility.

The garden is characterized by its lush greenery and a variety of trees, including maples, pines, and cherry blossoms. Seasonal changes bring new colors and beauty to the garden, with spring cherry blossoms and autumn foliage being particularly popular times to visit. The traditional tea house, nestled among the trees, is an ideal spot to take a break and enjoy the view.

Murin-an Garden also features a two-story wooden villa that served as Yamagata's residence, which is now open to the public. The villa's architecture is representative of the Meiji Period and offers a glimpse into the lifestyle of Japan's elite during that time.

To reach Murin-an Garden, visitors can take the Kyoto City Bus to the Kumano Jinja-mae bus stop, followed by a short walk. The garden is open year-round and requires an admission fee. Visiting Murin-an Garden is an opportunity to experience the artistry and craftsmanship of traditional Japanese landscape design while enjoying the peaceful atmosphere of this historic and picturesque oasis.

By exploring Kyoto's gardens and parks, you can discover the city's deep connection to nature, experience the artistry of Japanese landscaping, and enjoy moments of peace and tranquility in these serene spaces.

CHAPTER FOUR

Experiencing Kyoto's Food and Drink

In this chapter, we will delve into the rich culinary landscape of Kyoto, where traditional and modern flavors come together to offer a unique gastronomic experience. Kyoto is well-known for its exceptional food culture, which has been shaped by its history as Japan's ancient capital, its abundant natural resources, and its sophisticated artistry. From traditional Kaiseki Ryori to street food, tea ceremonies to trendy cafes, Kyoto has something for every palate and preference.

Traditional Kyoto Cuisine

Kyoto's cuisine, known as Kyo-ryori, has a long and rich history that has been influenced by its status as Japan's ancient capital, its Buddhist and imperial traditions, and its abundant local produce. Traditional Kyoto cuisine is characterized by its emphasis on seasonality, artful presentation, and delicate flavors. Here are some of the highlights of traditional Kyoto cuisine:

- Kaiseki Ryori: Kaiseki is a traditional multi-course Japanese meal that showcases the finest seasonal ingredients and culinary techniques. Kaiseki meals typically include a variety of small dishes, such as appetizers, sashimi, grilled and simmered dishes, rice, and dessert. The dishes are carefully prepared and presented, often using exquisite tableware and intricate garnishes. Kaiseki is considered the pinnacle of Japanese haute cuisine and can be enjoyed at high-end restaurants or ryokan (Japanese-style inns).

- Shojin Ryori: Shojin Ryori is a vegetarian cuisine that originated from the Buddhist temples in Kyoto. This style of cooking emphasizes the use of seasonal vegetables, tofu, and grains, and avoids meat and fish. Shojin Ryori is known for its delicate flavors, simple preparation methods, and balanced nutrition. You can experience Shojin Ryori at temple lodgings or specialized restaurants around Kyoto.

- Obanzai Ryori: Obanzai is Kyoto's home-style cooking, characterized by simple, comforting dishes made with locally-sourced ingredients.

Obanzai dishes often include simmered vegetables, pickles, and miso soup, with a focus on using seasonal produce and minimizing waste. Many Kyoto restaurants and izakaya (Japanese pubs) offer a selection of Obanzai dishes, giving visitors a taste of Kyoto's everyday cuisine.

- Yuba: Yuba, or tofu skin, is a specialty of Kyoto and is made by skimming the delicate skin that forms on the surface of boiling soy milk. Yuba can be enjoyed in various forms, such as fresh, dried, or deep-fried, and is often used in soups, salads, and sushi. There are numerous restaurants and shops in Kyoto that specialize in yuba dishes.

- Kyoto Sushi: Kyoto-style sushi, known as Kyozushi or Sabazushi, is distinct from the more familiar nigiri sushi found in other parts of Japan. Kyozushi typically features cured or cooked fish, such as mackerel or saba, pressed onto vinegar-seasoned rice and wrapped in kombu (kelp). This style of sushi has a longer shelf life and is perfect for enjoying on the go or as part of a bento (boxed meal).

When visiting Kyoto, be sure to explore the city's traditional cuisine, which offers a unique and unforgettable dining experience that reflects the region's history, culture, and natural bounty.

Street Food and Markets

Kyoto's street food scene and local markets offer a variety of delicious and affordable options for travelers to enjoy. The city is known for its lively markets and food stalls, where you can sample a range of traditional Japanese snacks, sweets, and other culinary delights. Here are some must-visit places and street foods to try in Kyoto:

- Nishiki Market: Known as "Kyoto's Kitchen," Nishiki Market is a bustling shopping street that offers an array of fresh produce, seafood, and prepared foods. The market is lined with over 100 shops and stalls, many of which have been in business for generations. Be sure to try some of the market's signature snacks, such as skewered octopus with quail eggs, soy milk doughnuts, and pickled vegetables.

- Pontocho Alley: Pontocho Alley is a narrow, atmospheric street along the Kamo River that is home to numerous bars, restaurants, and food stalls. This is a great place to sample yakitori (grilled chicken skewers), takoyaki (octopus balls), and okonomiyaki (savory pancakes), while enjoying the lively ambiance of the alley.

- Fushimi Inari Taisha: The area around Fushimi Inari Taisha is known for its street food vendors, who offer a variety of tasty treats for visitors to enjoy. Some popular options include inarizushi (rice-stuffed tofu pockets), kitsune udon (noodle soup with fried tofu), and yuba (tofu skin) dishes.

- Gion District: The historic Gion District is not only famous for its geisha culture but also for its street food scene. Stroll through the narrow streets and sample traditional Japanese sweets like matcha ice cream, dango (rice dumplings), and taiyaki (fish-shaped waffles filled with sweet bean paste).

- Kiyomizu-dera Temple Area: The streets leading up to Kiyomizu-dera Temple are lined with shops and food stalls offering a range of local snacks and souvenirs. Popular options include yatsuhashi (a sweet, cinnamon-flavored rice cracker), green tea-flavored treats, and Mitarashi dango (rice dumplings covered in a sweet soy glaze).

Exploring Kyoto's street food scene and local markets is an excellent way to experience the city's diverse culinary offerings, discover new flavors, and immerse yourself in Kyoto's vibrant culture.

Tea Culture and Sweets

Kyoto is renowned for its rich tea culture, which dates back to the early Heian Period (794-1185). The city is famous for its matcha, a finely ground green tea powder, and the tea ceremony, a traditional ritual of preparing and serving tea. Kyoto is also home to a variety of traditional Japanese sweets, which are often enjoyed in tandem with a cup of tea. Here are some insights into Kyoto's tea culture and sweets:

- Matcha: Kyoto's Uji region is famous for producing some of the finest matcha in Japan. The vibrant green tea powder is known for its earthy flavor and numerous health benefits. Matcha is not only enjoyed as a beverage but is also used as a key ingredient in many sweets and dishes, such as matcha ice cream, matcha latte, and matcha soba noodles.

- Tea Ceremony: The Japanese tea ceremony, also known as "chanoyu" or "sado," is an important aspect of Kyoto's tea culture. The ceremony is a highly choreographed ritual of preparing and serving matcha, with an emphasis on harmony, respect, and tranquility. Visitors to Kyoto can attend tea ceremonies or take lessons to learn about the art and philosophy behind this ancient practice.

- Wagashi: Wagashi are traditional Japanese sweets often served with tea. These confections are crafted with great attention to detail and are made from natural ingredients such as mochi (rice cake), anko (sweet red bean paste), and fruit. Some popular types of wagashi include daifuku, dorayaki, and yatsuhashi, which are often flavored with matcha, azuki beans, or seasonal fruits.

- Tea Houses and Cafes: Kyoto is home to numerous traditional tea houses and modern cafes, where visitors can enjoy a relaxing cup of tea and a variety of sweets. Some famous tea houses in

Kyoto include Ippodo Tea, which has been serving high-quality tea for over 300 years, and the historic Camellia Tea House. For a modern twist, check out the numerous cafes offering matcha lattes, parfaits, and other innovative tea-based treats.

- Tea Festivals and Events: Kyoto hosts several tea-related events throughout the year, such as the annual Uji Tea Festival, which celebrates the city's tea culture with parades, tea-tasting sessions, and tea-picking experiences.

Exploring Kyoto's tea culture and sweets allows visitors to appreciate the city's long-standing traditions, savor unique flavors, and experience the artistry and craftsmanship that goes into creating these delightful treats.

Sake and Craft Beer

Kyoto is known not only for its tea culture but also for its sake and burgeoning craft beer scene. With its high-quality water sources and a long history of brewing, the city offers a wide range of drinking experiences for visitors to explore. Here are some details on Kyoto's sake and craft beer offerings:

- Sake: Kyoto is home to the Fushimi District, one of Japan's most famous sake-producing regions. The area boasts a high concentration of sake breweries, thanks to its pristine water sources, which are essential for brewing high-quality sake. Fushimi's sake is known for its smooth, mellow taste, and there are numerous breweries open for tours and tastings. Some popular breweries in the area include Gekkeikan Okura Sake Museum, Kizakura, and Sudo Honke.

- Sake Tastings and Tours: Many sake breweries in Kyoto offer guided tours, providing insight into the history and brewing process of sake. Visitors can learn about the various types of sake, such as junmai, ginjo, and daiginjo, and enjoy sake tastings. Some breweries also have onsite shops where you can purchase your favorite bottles to take home.

- Craft Beer: Over the past few years, Kyoto has seen a growth in its craft beer scene, with several microbreweries and craft beer bars opening throughout the city. These establishments offer a diverse selection of Japanese and international craft beers, showcasing unique flavors and brewing techniques. Some popular craft beer spots in Kyoto include Kyoto Brewing Company, Before9, and Beer Komachi.

- Beer Festivals and Events: Kyoto hosts several beer-related events throughout the year, such as the annual Kyoto Craft Beer Festival, which features local and international breweries, food vendors, and live music. These events provide an excellent opportunity to sample a variety of beers and engage with Kyoto's vibrant craft beer community.

- Pairing Food and Drink: When exploring Kyoto's sake and craft beer scene, don't forget to indulge in the city's culinary delights. Many breweries and bars offer food menus designed to complement their beverages, featuring traditional Japanese dishes, izakaya-style snacks, and international fare.

Whether you're a sake connoisseur, a craft beer enthusiast, or simply curious about Kyoto's brewing culture, there's no shortage of opportunities to discover and enjoy the city's diverse drink offerings.

Fine Dining and International Cuisine

Kyoto is not only famous for its traditional Japanese cuisine but also offers an exquisite selection of fine dining and international cuisine options. The city's culinary scene has embraced global flavors while maintaining its unique Kyoto touch. Here are some fine dining and international cuisine options to consider during your stay in Kyoto:

Kikunoi: This Michelin-starred restaurant is known for its exceptional kaiseki (traditional Japanese multi-course meal) dining experience. Located in a beautiful Japanese-style building with serene gardens, Kikunoi offers a memorable dining experience with seasonal ingredients and stunning presentation.

Address: 459 Shimokawara-cho, Higashiyama-ku, Kyoto

La Biographie: If you are craving French cuisine, La Biographie is a fantastic option. This intimate, Michelin-starred restaurant offers an elegant atmosphere and an exquisite menu featuring French dishes with a Japanese twist. The chef's passion for using local ingredients ensures a unique and delicious dining experience.

Address: 570-107 Gionmachi Minamigawa, Higashiyama-ku, Kyoto

Il Ghiottone: For Italian cuisine lovers, Il Ghiottone is a must-visit. With a focus on using Kyoto's finest ingredients, the chef creates Italian dishes with a Japanese sensibility. The restaurant's modern, stylish interior adds to the refined dining experience.

Address: 1F Yonemoto Building, 318-2 Izumiya-cho, Nijodori Sanjo-agaru, Nakagyo-ku, Kyoto

Shoraian: This restaurant is located in the picturesque Arashiyama district and specializes in tofu-based dishes. Offering stunning views of the Hozu River, Shoraian is an excellent choice for those looking to experience a traditional Kyoto meal in a serene setting.

Address: 4 Sagaogurayama Tabuchiyama-cho, Ukyo-ku, Kyoto

Tousuiro: Another fantastic option for tofu lovers is Tousuiro. This elegant restaurant is dedicated to creating innovative and flavorful tofu dishes that will change your perception of this humble ingredient. With beautiful presentation and impeccable service, Tousuiro offers a memorable dining experience.

Address: Kiyamachi-dori, Bukkoji-agaru, Nakagyo-ku, Kyoto

Kyoto's international cuisine scene is thriving and diverse, providing travelers with a wide range of options to suit all tastes. From authentic Italian and French cuisine to innovative fusion dishes, Kyoto offers a culinary adventure that goes beyond its traditional Japanese roots.

Vegetarian and Vegan Options

Kyoto is a city that caters well to vegetarians and vegans, offering a variety of traditional and contemporary dining options. The city's Buddhist history and the influence of temple cuisine have contributed to the development of a rich vegetarian and vegan food culture. Here are some details on Kyoto's vegetarian and vegan offerings:

- Shojin Ryori: Shojin ryori is a type of traditional vegetarian cuisine that originated in Buddhist temples. This style of cooking uses seasonal ingredients and avoids meat, fish, and other animal products. Shojin ryori focuses on the balance of flavors and colors, creating dishes that are as visually appealing as they are delicious. Some well-known shojin ryori restaurants in Kyoto include Shigetsu at Tenryu-ji Temple, Izusen at Daitoku-ji Temple, and Shojin Ryori Toufuya.

- Tofu and Yuba: Kyoto is famous for its high-quality tofu and yuba (tofu skin), which are often used as protein sources in vegetarian and vegan dishes. The city has numerous tofu specialty restaurants that serve a variety of tofu-based dishes, such as yudofu (simmered tofu), agedashi tofu (deep-fried tofu), and tofu steak. Some popular tofu restaurants include Tousuiro, Okutan, and Yubasen.

- Veggie-friendly Japanese Eateries: Many traditional Japanese restaurants in Kyoto offer vegetarian and vegan options or can adjust their dishes to accommodate dietary restrictions. For instance, some kaiseki (multi-course) restaurants have vegetarian menus, while soba and udon noodle shops often offer vegetable-based broths and toppings. Don't hesitate to ask the staff for vegetarian or vegan options when dining out.

- Vegetarian and Vegan Cafés and Restaurants: Kyoto is home to several dedicated vegetarian and vegan eateries that serve a variety of dishes, from Japanese to international cuisine. Some popular options include Veg Out, Ain Soph.Journey Kyoto, and Padma. These establishments often use organic and locally sourced ingredients, creating healthy and flavorful meals.

- Veggie-friendly Convenience Stores and Supermarkets: For travelers on a budget or in need of a quick meal, convenience stores and supermarkets in Kyoto often stock a range of vegetarian and vegan products. Look for onigiri (rice balls) with vegetable fillings, inari sushi (tofu pockets filled with rice), or pre-packaged salads and bento boxes.

With its diverse range of vegetarian and vegan dining options, Kyoto is a city that caters to various dietary preferences and needs, ensuring that all visitors can enjoy the flavors of Japan's cultural capital.

CHAPTER FIVE

Shopping and Souvenirs in Kyoto

In this chapter, we will explore the various shopping opportunities in Kyoto, from traditional crafts to modern boutiques, and highlight the best places to find unique souvenirs that capture the essence of this cultural capital.

Traditional Crafts and Handicrafts

Kyoto is renowned for its exquisite traditional crafts, such as pottery, lacquerware, and textiles. You can find these beautiful items in specialized shops and galleries throughout the city.

- Kiyomizu-yaki and Kyo-yaki Pottery: Kiyomizu-yaki and Kyo-yaki are two famous types of Kyoto ceramics with a history of more than 400 years. They are known for their intricate designs and vivid colors. You can find these beautiful pieces of pottery in specialized shops around Kyoto, particularly in the Gojozaka district near Kiyomizu-dera Temple.

- Lacquerware (Shikki): Kyoto's lacquerware is known for its exceptional quality and craftsmanship. With a history dating back more than a thousand years, Kyoto Shikki is characterized by intricate designs and a high degree of artistic expression. Some popular lacquerware items include bowls, trays, and chopsticks. You can find Kyoto Shikki in shops and galleries throughout the city, especially in the Teramachi and Nishiki Market areas.

- Nishijin Textiles: Nishijin is a district in Kyoto famous for its traditional textile weaving. This ancient craft has been passed down through generations and is known for its high-quality silk fabrics, used for kimonos, obi sashes, and interior decorations. Visit the Nishijin Textile Center to learn about the weaving process, watch demonstrations, and shop for unique textile products.

- Kyoto Folding Fans (Sensu): Folding fans are a traditional Japanese accessory, and Kyoto's sensu are considered some of the finest in Japan. They are made from high-quality bamboo and washi paper, often featuring delicate hand-painted designs. You can find beautiful Kyoto folding fans in various souvenir shops and specialty stores around the city, such as Miyawaki Baisen-an.

- Bamboo Crafts: Kyoto's Arashiyama district is famous for its bamboo groves, which provide the raw material for various bamboo crafts, including baskets, trays, and utensils. You can find these items in shops around Arashiyama and throughout Kyoto.

- Handmade Washi Paper: Kyoto is known for its high-quality handmade washi paper, used for various purposes such as calligraphy, origami, and even interior design. Visit the Kamiji Kakimoto shop in Teramachi shopping district or Ozu Washi near Nishiki Market to find an impressive selection of washi paper products.

When shopping for traditional crafts and handicrafts in Kyoto, make sure to visit specialized shops, galleries, and artisan workshops to learn more about the history and techniques behind each craft. This will not only provide a deeper appreciation for the items but also ensure that you are purchasing authentic, high-quality products.

Textiles and Kimono

Kyoto's textile industry has a long history, with the city being a hub for silk production and weaving. As a result, Kyoto is an ideal place to shop for kimono, yukata (summer kimono), and other traditional clothing. You can find both new and vintage kimonos at various price points in the city's numerous kimono shops

- Nishijin Textiles: As mentioned earlier, Nishijin is a district in Kyoto famous for its traditional textile weaving. With a history of over 1,200 years, Nishijin weaving is characterized by intricate patterns and the use of high-quality silk. The woven textiles are often used to create kimonos, obi sashes, and other traditional clothing items, as well as interior decorations. Visit the Nishijin Textile Center to learn more about this craft, watch live demonstrations, and shop for Nishijin products.

- Kyo-Yuzen: Kyo-Yuzen is a traditional Kyoto dyeing technique used to create colorful and intricate patterns on kimonos and other textiles. This technique involves hand-painting or stencil-dyeing designs onto the fabric and is known for its vibrant colors and fine details. To explore Kyo-Yuzen textiles and kimonos, visit specialized shops such as Marumasu Nishimuraya or Chiso in the downtown Kyoto area.

- Shibori: Shibori is a Japanese tie-dyeing technique that has been practiced in Kyoto for centuries. It involves folding, twisting, and tying fabric before dyeing it, resulting in unique patterns and textures. You can find beautiful shibori textiles and kimonos in specialty shops around the city, such as Kyoto Shibori Museum and Gallery.

- Kimono Rental and Dressing Experiences: While in Kyoto, consider renting a kimono and wearing it as you explore the city's historic streets and temples. There are numerous kimono rental shops throughout the city, particularly in the Gion and Higashiyama districts. Some shops also offer professional dressing services, so you can experience the traditional way of putting on a kimono. Additionally, you may find kimono photography packages, allowing you to capture memorable moments in traditional Japanese attire.

- Kimono Shopping: If you wish to purchase a kimono as a souvenir or gift, there are various options to consider. New kimonos can be quite expensive, but you can find more affordable vintage or pre-owned kimonos in shops such as Komehyo and Chicago Harajuku. These stores often carry a wide selection of kimonos, obi sashes, and accessories.

When exploring textiles and kimonos in Kyoto, take the time to learn about the different techniques, materials, and history behind each piece. This will give you a deeper appreciation for the craftsmanship and artistry involved in creating these beautiful garments and textiles.

Tea and Sweets

Kyoto is famous for its matcha (green tea) and traditional Japanese sweets (wagashi). Visit tea shops and confectioneries like Ippodo, Marukyu Koyamaen, and Kanshundo to taste and purchase high-quality tea and sweets. Many of these shops offer beautifully wrapped gift sets that make perfect souvenirs.

- Matcha: Kyoto is renowned for its matcha, a finely ground green tea powder used in traditional Japanese tea ceremonies and as a popular ingredient in sweets. The Uji area, located just south of Kyoto, is particularly famous for its high-quality matcha. Visit tea shops such as Ippodo, Marukyu-Koyamaen, or Tsujiri to buy premium matcha powder and other tea-related products.

- Tea Ceremony Experiences: To immerse yourself in Japanese tea culture, consider participating in a traditional tea ceremony. During the ceremony, you will learn about the history, etiquette, and techniques of preparing and serving matcha. Tea houses such as Camellia, En, and Ju-An offer tea ceremony experiences for visitors.

- Wagashi: Wagashi are traditional Japanese confections, often made from sweetened bean paste and served with tea. Kyoto is known for its delicate and artful wagashi, which are often inspired by the seasons and local culture. Visit venerable confectionery shops like Kameya Yoshinaga, Kanshundo, and Tsuruya Yoshinobu to sample an array of wagashi, including the famous yatsuhashi, a cinnamon-flavored rice cake filled with sweet bean paste.

- Green Tea Ice Cream and Parfaits: Kyoto's love for matcha extends to its desserts, with green tea ice cream and parfaits being particularly popular. You'll find many cafes and ice cream shops offering these treats, with some of the best found at Gion Tsujiri, Nana's Green Tea, and Kyo Hayashiya.

- Japanese Sweets Cafes: In addition to traditional tea houses, Kyoto is home to numerous cafes that specialize in Japanese sweets. These establishments often offer a modern twist on classic confections, pairing them with a variety of teas, coffees, and other beverages. Some popular cafes to try are Kagizen Yoshifusa, Kyo Baum, and Toraya Karyo Ichijo.

- Kaiseki Ryori: For a truly indulgent experience, consider trying kaiseki ryori, a traditional multi-course Japanese meal often served in high-end restaurants and ryokans. Kaiseki menus typically include a variety of small, artfully presented dishes that showcase local and seasonal ingredients. Many kaiseki meals end with a beautifully crafted wagashi and a cup of matcha tea. Some well-regarded kaiseki establishments in Kyoto include Kikunoi, Kitcho Arashiyama, and Gion Suetomo.

When exploring Kyoto's tea and sweets scene, be sure to savor the delicate flavors and artistry that define this essential aspect of Japanese culture.

Shopping Districts and Malls

Kyoto offers a mix of shopping districts, malls, and department stores, catering to a variety of tastes and budgets.

- Shijo-Kawaramachi: This bustling shopping district, located at the intersection of Shijo Street and Kawaramachi Street, is the heart of Kyoto's retail scene. Here, you'll find a mix of department stores, fashion boutiques, and souvenir shops. Notable stores in the area include Daimaru, Takashimaya, and OPA.

- Teramachi and Shinkyogoku Shopping Arcades: These two parallel shopping streets are home to a variety of shops selling clothing, accessories, souvenirs, and traditional crafts. Both arcades are covered, making them a convenient destination for shopping on rainy days. Don't miss the Kyoto Handicraft Center and the flagship store of Tsujiri, a famous matcha brand.

- Nishiki Market: Known as Kyoto's Kitchen, this narrow, covered market is lined with more than 100 shops and stalls offering fresh produce, seafood, and local delicacies. It's a great place to buy food souvenirs, such as pickles, sweets, and tea.

- Kyoto Station Area: The area surrounding Kyoto Station is home to several large shopping malls, including Kyoto Tower Sando, Porta, and The Cube. These malls feature a mix of Japanese and international brands, as well as restaurants and entertainment options.

- Kyoto BAL: Located in the Shijo-Kawaramachi area, Kyoto BAL is a modern shopping mall offering a selection of trendy fashion, lifestyle goods, and restaurants. It's a good place to find the latest Japanese trends and international brands.

- Fujii Daimaru: This department store, also in the Shijo-Kawaramachi area, is known for its selection of traditional Japanese goods, including kimono, tea, and pottery. It's an excellent destination for finding high-quality souvenirs and gifts.

- AEON Mall Kyoto: Located a short train ride from Kyoto Station, AEON Mall Kyoto is a large shopping complex with numerous stores, restaurants, and entertainment options. It offers a mix of Japanese and international brands, making it a popular destination for locals and tourists alike.

- Kitayama and Demachiyanagi: These two neighborhoods, located in the northern part of the city, offer a more laid-back shopping experience. You'll find a mix of artisan shops, galleries, and cafes, along with a relaxed atmosphere perfect for leisurely browsing.

When exploring Kyoto's shopping districts and malls, be sure to take your time and enjoy the diverse array of goods and experiences available in this culturally rich city.

Flea Markets and Antique Shops

Kyoto is home to several flea markets and antique shops, offering a unique opportunity to find one-of-a-kind treasures and vintage items.

The two most famous flea markets are the Kobo-san Market (held on the 21st of each month at To-ji Temple) and the Tenjin-san Market (held on the 25th of each month at Kitano Tenmangu Shrine). These markets are great places to find traditional crafts, ceramics, textiles, and antiques at reasonable prices.

- Kobo-san Market: Held on the 21st of every month at To-ji Temple, Kobo-san Market is a famous flea market where you can find a wide range of items, from antiques and traditional crafts to clothing, ceramics, and food. With over 1,000 stalls, it's an excellent place to search for unique souvenirs and experience the local atmosphere.

- Tenjin-san Market: Similar to Kobo-san Market, Tenjin-san Market is held on the 25th of every month at Kitano Tenmangu Shrine. This market offers an extensive selection of antiques, vintage items, traditional crafts, and food. It's a popular destination for both locals and tourists looking for one-of-a-kind finds.

- Aoniyoshi: Aoniyoshi is a well-known antique shop in Kyoto that specializes in ceramics, lacquerware, and other traditional Japanese crafts. Located in the Gion district, this shop offers a carefully curated selection of high-quality items, making it an ideal destination for serious collectors and casual shoppers alike.

- Kyoto Antique Mall: Located near Shijo-Kawaramachi, Kyoto Antique Mall is a multi-story building filled with various antique dealers offering a diverse range of items, including pottery, textiles, furniture, and art. It's an excellent place to browse and discover unique treasures from Japan's past.

- Furukawacho Shopping Street: This charming shopping street, located near the Higashiyama district, is home to several antique shops and traditional craft stores. With a more relaxed atmosphere than some of the larger shopping areas, it's a pleasant place to spend an afternoon browsing for unique items.

- Gion Antique Fair: Held on the first Sunday of every month (except January) in the Gion district, the Gion Antique Fair offers a variety of antiques, vintage items, and traditional crafts from a range of vendors. It's an excellent opportunity to find unique souvenirs and experience the local flea market culture.

- Chion-ji Temple Handicraft Market: Held on the 15th of every month at Chion-ji Temple, this market showcases handmade crafts from local artisans. While not specifically an antique market, you can still find unique, traditional items, along with a variety of crafts and food.

When visiting flea markets and antique shops in Kyoto, remember to keep an open mind and be prepared to haggle for the best prices. These markets and shops offer a fascinating insight into Japanese culture and history, making them a must-visit for anyone interested in discovering the treasures of Kyoto.

In this chapter, we have provided an overview of the shopping scene in Kyoto and highlighted some of the best places to find unique souvenirs that will remind you of your time in Japan's cultural capital. Happy shopping!

CHAPTER SIX

Day Trips from Kyoto

Kyoto's central location in the Kansai region makes it an ideal base for exploring the surrounding areas. There are numerous day trips available, allowing visitors to experience a diverse range of landscapes, historical sites, and cultural attractions. Here are some of the most popular day trip destinations from Kyoto

Nara

Nara, the ancient capital of Japan before Kyoto, is a city steeped in history and cultural heritage. Located less than an hour away from Kyoto by train, Nara is a popular day trip destination for travelers. With a range of temples, shrines, and parks, Nara offers visitors a glimpse into Japan's past.

- Todai-ji Temple: Todai-ji is Nara's most famous and significant temple, housing the Great Buddha (Daibutsu), one of the largest bronze Buddha statues in the world. The temple was constructed in the 8th century and has since been designated a UNESCO World Heritage Site. The massive wooden structure, the Daibutsuden (Great Buddha Hall), which contains the Great Buddha, is a marvel in itself.

- Nara Park: Nara Park is a large public park in the heart of Nara, spanning over 660 hectares. It is home to over a thousand semi-wild deer that roam freely and are considered the messengers of the gods in the Shinto religion. Visitors can feed the deer with special deer crackers (shika senbei) available for purchase at the park.

- Kasuga Taisha Shrine: Another UNESCO World Heritage Site, Kasuga Taisha Shrine is Nara's most important Shinto shrine. Established in the 8th century, it is famous for its thousands of stone and bronze lanterns donated by worshippers over the years. The lanterns are lit twice a year during the Mantoro Lantern Festivals in February and August.

- Kofuku-ji Temple: Kofuku-ji is a Buddhist temple complex that was once among the powerful Seven Great Temples of Nara. The five-story pagoda, one of the tallest wooden structures in Japan, is a striking feature of the temple complex.

- Naramachi: Naramachi is the historical merchant district of Nara, featuring traditional wooden townhouses (machiya), narrow streets, and small shops. It is a perfect place to wander and soak up the atmosphere of old Nara.

- Isuien Garden: Isuien is a traditional Japanese garden with a serene atmosphere, featuring manicured lawns, ponds, bridges, and tea houses. The garden offers stunning views of the surrounding temples and hills, making it an ideal spot for a quiet stroll.

- Horyu-ji Temple: Located slightly outside Nara city, Horyu-ji Temple is another UNESCO World Heritage Site and one of the oldest wooden structures in the world. The temple houses a collection of priceless Buddhist art, including statues and wall paintings.

With its rich history, ancient temples, and natural beauty, Nara offers a fascinating day trip for travelers looking to explore Japan's cultural heritage beyond Kyoto.

Osaka

Osaka is Japan's third-largest city and a bustling metropolis known for its vibrant food culture, modern architecture, and lively atmosphere. Located just 15 minutes by shinkansen (bullet train) or about an hour by regular train from Kyoto, Osaka makes for an excellent day trip destination for travelers.

- Dotonbori: Dotonbori is the entertainment and food heart of Osaka, with its iconic neon signs, bustling shopping arcades, and numerous restaurants and street food vendors. A stroll along the Dotonbori Canal is a must-do for visitors, with the famous Glico Running Man sign and Kani Doraku crab sign being popular photo spots.

- Osaka Castle: Osaka Castle is a historic landmark and symbol of the city. The castle was built in the late 16th century by Toyotomi Hideyoshi, a powerful Japanese warlord. Today, the castle houses a museum displaying artifacts and exhibits related to the history of the castle and the city. The castle park, with its beautiful gardens and moats, is a popular spot for picnics and cherry blossom viewing in spring.

- Universal Studios Japan: This world-renowned theme park offers a fun-filled day for families and fans of Hollywood movies, with themed attractions and shows based on popular films and characters, such as Harry Potter, Jurassic Park, and Minions.

- Umeda Sky Building: The Umeda Sky Building is a modern architectural marvel consisting of two 40-story towers connected at the top by the Floating Garden Observatory. The observatory offers 360-degree panoramic views of Osaka, making it a popular spot for taking in the city skyline, especially at sunset.

- Shinsekai: Shinsekai is a nostalgic and colorful neighborhood that was designed to resemble New York and Paris in the early 20th century. The area is famous for its kushikatsu (deep-fried skewers) restaurants, retro atmosphere, and the Tsutenkaku Tower, a symbol of Osaka's post-war rebirth.

- Shitenno-ji Temple: As one of Japan's oldest Buddhist temples, Shitenno-ji was founded by

Prince Shotoku in the 6th century. The temple complex includes a five-story pagoda, a main hall, and a treasure house, displaying artifacts from the temple's history.

- Kuromon Ichiba Market: Known as "Osaka's kitchen," Kuromon Ichiba Market is a lively food market offering a wide range of fresh seafood, produce, and ready-to-eat dishes. It's an excellent spot to sample Osaka's famous street food, such as takoyaki (octopus balls) and okonomiyaki (savory pancakes).

Osaka is a dynamic city with a rich history and modern attractions, offering visitors a unique blend of old and new Japan. From historical landmarks to contemporary architecture and a buzzing food scene, Osaka has something for everyone.

Kobe

Kobe is a charming port city located just over an hour away from Kyoto by train, making it an ideal destination for a day trip. Known for its picturesque harbor, diverse cultural influences, and delicious cuisine, Kobe has a range of attractions that make it worth visiting.

- Kobe Harborland: This popular waterfront area is home to a variety of shopping, dining, and entertainment options. Kobe Harborland features the iconic red Kobe Port Tower, which offers panoramic views of the city and harbor from its observation deck. At night, the area comes alive with illuminated buildings and a dazzling Ferris wheel.

- Nankinmachi (Kobe Chinatown): As a testament to Kobe's international character, Nankinmachi is a lively and colorful neighborhood filled with Chinese restaurants, shops, and street food vendors. This bustling area is a great place to sample authentic Chinese cuisine and shop for unique souvenirs.

- Meriken Park: Meriken Park is a scenic waterfront park that offers stunning views of Kobe's skyline and port. The park is home to the Kobe Maritime Museum, which showcases the city's maritime history and technological advancements, and the poignant Kobe Earthquake Memorial, commemorating the devastating 1995 Great Hanshin Earthquake.

- Ikuta Shrine: Ikuta Shrine is one of Japan's oldest Shinto shrines, with a history dating back over a thousand years. Surrounded by lush greenery, the shrine offers a peaceful respite from the city's hustle and bustle. The shrine is particularly beautiful during the cherry blossom season in spring.

- Kobe Nunobiki Herb Gardens: Accessible by a scenic ropeway, the Kobe Nunobiki Herb Gardens are a delightful attraction featuring over 200 varieties of herbs and flowers. Visitors can stroll through the beautifully landscaped gardens, enjoy the panoramic views of Kobe, and even sample herbal teas and dishes at the garden's cafe.

- Kobe Beef: Kobe is world-renowned for its delicious and tender Kobe beef, which comes from the local Tajima strain of wagyu cattle. Be sure to try this delicacy at one of the city's many specialized restaurants, where you can enjoy the melt-in-your-mouth experience of perfectly cooked Kobe beef.

- Sake Breweries: Kobe's Nada district is one of Japan's most prominent sake-producing regions. Several breweries offer tours and tastings, giving visitors an opportunity to learn about the brewing process and sample various types of sake.

- Kobe is a captivating city that offers a unique blend of cultural influences, natural beauty, and delectable cuisine. With its picturesque harbor, diverse attractions, and friendly atmosphere, Kobe is a perfect day trip destination for travelers exploring the Kansai region.

Himeji

Himeji is a city located in the Hyogo Prefecture of Japan, approximately 90 minutes away from Kyoto by train. It is best known for its magnificent Himeji Castle, a UNESCO World Heritage Site. The city offers a range of attractions that make it an excellent choice for a day trip from Kyoto.

- Himeji Castle: Also known as the "White Heron Castle" due to its brilliant white exterior, Himeji Castle is a stunning example of Japanese castle architecture and one of the few original castles remaining in the country. The castle, which dates back to the 14th century, features a multi-story main keep and several other buildings, all surrounded by fortifications and moats. Visitors can explore the castle grounds, climb the main keep for panoramic views of the city, and learn about the castle's history in the on-site museum.

- Koko-en Garden: Located adjacent to Himeji Castle, Koko-en Garden is a beautiful Japanese landscape garden that was constructed in 1992 to commemorate the 100th anniversary of Himeji's city status. The garden consists of nine smaller gardens, each designed in a distinct traditional style. Visitors can enjoy the serene atmosphere, explore the tea houses, and participate in a traditional tea ceremony.

- Himeji City Zoo: This small zoo, situated near Himeji Castle, offers a fun and educational experience for visitors of all ages. The zoo is home to a variety of animals, including monkeys, penguins, and reptiles. It also features a petting zoo area where children can interact with smaller animals like rabbits and guinea pigs.

- Engyo-ji Temple: Engyo-ji Temple is a historic Buddhist temple complex located on Mount Shosha, just outside Himeji city. It can be reached via a scenic ropeway ride followed by a pleasant hike through the forest. The temple, founded in 966, features several impressive wooden buildings, including the main hall and a three-story pagoda. Engyo-ji Temple is also known as a filming location for the Hollywood movie "The Last Samurai."

- Himeji Central Park: This large recreational park offers a variety of activities, including an amusement park, a safari park, and a swimming pool. The amusement park features various rides and attractions suitable for both children and adults, while the safari park allows visitors to see animals such as lions, tigers, and bears up close from the safety of a vehicle.

- Shoshazan Ropeway: The Shoshazan Ropeway takes visitors from the base of Mount Shosha to the Engyo-ji Temple area. The ropeway offers stunning views of Himeji city and the surrounding countryside, making it a memorable experience.

Himeji provides an enjoyable day trip from Kyoto, offering a mix of historical attractions, natural beauty, and family-friendly activities. The centerpiece of any visit to Himeji is the impressive Himeji Castle, which is not to be missed.

Hiroshima and Miyajima Island

Hiroshima and Miyajima Island are popular day-trip destinations from Kyoto, offering visitors a mix of history, culture, and natural beauty. The journey from Kyoto to Hiroshima takes about 1 hour and 40 minutes to 2 hours by shinkansen (bullet train).

Hiroshima: Hiroshima is a city with a tragic history, as it was the first city to be attacked with an atomic bomb during World War II. Today, Hiroshima has been rebuilt and transformed into a vibrant and modern city with a strong focus on peace and harmony.

- Hiroshima Peace Memorial Park: This park is dedicated to the memory of those who perished during the atomic bombing of Hiroshima. It features several monuments and memorials, including the iconic A-Bomb Dome, the Children's Peace Monument, and the Hiroshima Peace Memorial Museum. The museum offers a moving and informative experience, detailing the events leading up to the bombing, its devastating effects, and the city's efforts to promote peace.

- Hiroshima Castle: Also known as Carp Castle, Hiroshima Castle is a reconstruction of the original castle that was destroyed during the atomic bombing. The castle serves as a museum, showcasing artifacts related to Hiroshima's history and samurai culture.

- Shukkei-en Garden: This beautiful Japanese landscape garden dates back to 1620 and is a peaceful oasis in the heart of Hiroshima. It features a central pond, tea houses, and several walking paths that allow visitors to explore the garden's varied scenery.

Miyajima Island: Miyajima Island, also known as Itsukushima, is a picturesque island located in the Seto Inland Sea, near Hiroshima. The island is best known for its floating torii gate and the Itsukushima Shrine. It takes about an hour to reach Miyajima from Hiroshima by train and ferry.

- Itsukushima Shrine: This UNESCO World Heritage Site is a Shinto shrine dedicated to the three daughters of the deity Susano-o. The shrine is famous for its iconic floating torii gate, which appears to be floating on the water during high tide. Visitors can also explore the shrine's various buildings and enjoy the stunning views of the Seto Inland Sea.

- Daisho-in Temple: Located at the base of Mount Misen, Daisho-in Temple is one of the most important Buddhist temples on Miyajima Island. The temple features several halls, pagodas, and statues, as well as a beautiful garden and a cave filled with Buddhist icons.

- Mount Misen: Mount Misen is the highest peak on Miyajima Island and offers breathtaking views of the Seto Inland Sea and surrounding islands. There are several hiking trails leading to the summit, or visitors can take the scenic Miyajima Ropeway for a more leisurely ascent.

- Omotesando Shopping Street: This lively street is lined with souvenir shops, restaurants, and food stalls, offering visitors a chance to sample local delicacies such as momiji manju (maple leaf-shaped cakes filled with sweet bean paste) and oysters.

Hiroshima and Miyajima Island provide visitors with a unique blend of history, culture, and natural beauty, making them ideal day-trip destinations from Kyoto.

Kinosaki Onsen

Kinosaki Onsen is a charming hot spring town located in Hyogo Prefecture, along the coast of the Sea of Japan. It is known for its traditional atmosphere, picturesque scenery, and a multitude of soothing hot springs. Kinosaki Onsen is a popular day trip or overnight destination from Kyoto, with the journey taking approximately 2.5 hours by train.

Here are some highlights of Kinosaki Onsen:

- Onsen-Hopping: Kinosaki Onsen is famous for its seven public hot spring bathhouses, or "sotoyu." Each bathhouse features unique architecture and offers a different atmosphere. Visitors can purchase a day pass allowing them to visit and enjoy all seven bathhouses. Most of the ryokans (traditional Japanese inns) in the area also have their private hot spring baths for guests.

- Kinosaki Ropeway: The Kinosaki Ropeway offers a scenic ride up Mount Daishi, providing stunning views of the town and the surrounding mountains. At the summit, there is an observation deck, a small temple, and a cafe. Visitors can also enjoy hiking trails around the area.

- Kinosaki Marine World: This aquarium is located near the coast and offers a variety of marine life exhibits, including dolphins, seals, and penguins. Visitors can watch dolphin and sea lion shows, as well as experience feeding and touching some of the animals.

- Strolling in Yukata: One of the most enjoyable activities in Kinosaki Onsen is strolling around the town in a traditional Japanese yukata (light cotton kimono) and wooden sandals provided by the ryokans. The town's quaint, willow-lined streets, bridges, and canals create a charming atmosphere perfect for leisurely walks.

- Local Cuisine: Kinosaki Onsen is known for its delicious seafood, particularly crab and Tajima beef. There are various restaurants and ryokans in the area offering these delicacies, as well as local sake and other Japanese dishes.

- Kinosaki Onsen Art Museum: The museum showcases a collection of contemporary Japanese art and ceramics, as well as a beautiful Japanese garden. The museum also hosts temporary exhibitions, featuring both local and international artists.

Visiting Kinosaki Onsen provides a relaxing and culturally immersive experience, allowing travelers to enjoy Japan's traditional hot spring culture and the town's charming atmosphere.

Uji

Uji is a small, historic city located in Kyoto Prefecture, just a short train ride (about 30 minutes) south of Kyoto. Uji is known for its rich cultural heritage, beautiful scenery, and most importantly, its production of high-quality green tea. The city has a tranquil atmosphere, making it a perfect day trip destination from Kyoto.

Here are some highlights of Uji:

- Byodo-in Temple: Byodo-in Temple is a UNESCO World Heritage Site and one of the most famous landmarks in Uji. The temple's Phoenix Hall, with its elegant architecture and stunning garden, is featured on the Japanese 10-yen coin. Inside the hall, you can find a large wooden statue of Amida Buddha, surrounded by a collection of smaller statues.

- Ujigami Shrine: Another UNESCO World Heritage Site, Ujigami Shrine is considered to be the oldest Shinto shrine in Japan. It is dedicated to Prince Uji-no-Wakiiratsuko, who is said to have established Uji as a city. The shrine features a unique architectural style, and its peaceful grounds are a great place to enjoy a leisurely stroll.

- Uji River: The scenic Uji River runs through the city, with several bridges connecting both sides of the river. A walk along the riverbank offers beautiful views and a chance to enjoy the tranquil atmosphere of the city. You can also take a relaxing boat tour to explore the river and learn about Uji's history and culture.

- Green Tea: Uji is famous for its high-quality green tea, particularly matcha, which is used in the traditional Japanese tea ceremony. You can find many tea shops in Uji selling various types of tea and tea-related products. You can also participate in tea-tasting events, tea ceremonies, or visit tea farms to learn about the tea-making process.

- Genji Monogatari Museum: Uji is closely related to "The Tale of Genji," one of the world's oldest and most important novels. The Genji Monogatari Museum is dedicated to the story and its author, Murasaki Shikibu. The museum features interactive exhibits, artifacts, and displays related to the novel, as well as a beautiful Japanese garden.

- Local Cuisine: In addition to tea, Uji offers a variety of local dishes and sweets featuring matcha. You can try matcha soba noodles, matcha ice cream, or various matcha-infused pastries and confections. The city is also known for its ayu (sweetfish), which is often grilled and served with rice.

Uji's historic sites, beautiful scenery, and unique culinary experiences make it a rewarding destination for those looking to explore beyond Kyoto's city center.

These day trips from Kyoto offer a diverse range of experiences, from ancient temples and shrines to bustling cities and relaxing hot springs. By venturing beyond Kyoto, visitors can gain a deeper understanding of Japan's rich history and culture, making their trip even more memorable.

How To Plan Your Day Trip

Planning a day trip from Kyoto to any of the nearby destinations requires some organization and research to make the most of your time. Here are some tips on how to plan your day trip:

- Research your destination: Before you set off, learn about the attractions, activities, and local customs of the place you plan to visit. Make a list of must-see spots and check their opening hours, entrance fees, and any other important information. This will help you prioritize your time and avoid any disappointments.

- Transportation: Look into the different transportation options from Kyoto to your chosen destination. Consider factors such as travel time, cost, and convenience. Check train or bus schedules and plan your departure time accordingly. If you plan to visit multiple locations in one day, research local transportation options within the destination, like buses or rental bicycles.

- Timing: Allocate enough time for each activity, keeping in mind that some attractions may require more time than others. Be realistic about what you can fit into a single day and try not to overextend yourself. Make sure to account for travel time, meal breaks, and some buffer time for unexpected events.

- Meal planning: Research local restaurants or cafes near the attractions you plan to visit. Find a few options for each meal and note their opening hours and any dietary restrictions they may cater to. Be open to trying local specialties and street food, which can be a great way to experience the local culture.

- Pack essentials: Bring a small backpack or bag with essentials like a water bottle, sunscreen, a hat, comfortable shoes, a light jacket or sweater, a camera, a portable phone charger, and some cash for entrance fees, meals, and souvenirs.

- Get an early start: To make the most of your day trip, it's a good idea to start early. This allows you to avoid crowds at popular attractions and gives you more time to explore at a relaxed pace.

- Be flexible: While it's important to have a plan, be prepared to adjust it as needed. You might discover a hidden gem or decide to spend more time at a particular attraction. Embrace the unexpected and enjoy the adventure.

By planning your day trip carefully and prioritizing the attractions and experiences that interest you the most, you can make the most of your time and create lasting memories of your visit to Japan's cultural capital and its surrounding areas.

CHAPTER SEVEN

Conclusion

As we conclude this comprehensive guide to exploring the best of Kyoto, Japan's cultural capital, it is important to reflect on the experiences, memories, and discoveries that await you. Kyoto is a city that effortlessly blends the past and the present, offering travelers a unique opportunity to immerse themselves in a rich cultural tapestry that has been woven over centuries.

In Kyoto, you will wander through ancient temples and shrines, marvel at the exquisite beauty of its gardens and parks, and indulge in the refined flavors of traditional Japanese cuisine. The city's vibrant shopping districts and bustling markets provide ample opportunity to find unique souvenirs and immerse yourself in the local arts and crafts. Day trips to nearby destinations will further enrich your understanding of Japan's history and culture.

As you prepare for your journey, remember to be present and mindful of the experiences that unfold before you. Kyoto is a city that rewards those who take the time to truly appreciate its subtleties and nuances. The quiet moments you spend strolling along the Philosopher's Path, the delicate taste of matcha tea in a traditional tea house, and the mesmerizing dance of a geisha in Gion are all integral to understanding the essence of Kyoto.

Throughout your travels, be respectful of local customs and etiquette, and embrace the opportunity to learn from the people you meet. The warmth and hospitality of Kyoto's residents will leave a lasting impression on your heart and mind.

Lastly, remember that your journey to Kyoto is not merely about ticking off a list of attractions or snapping the perfect photograph. It is about discovering a deeper connection to the city's history, culture, and spirit. As you leave Kyoto, carry with you the memories, lessons, and insights gained from your time in this enchanting city, and let them serve as a reminder of the timeless charm of Japan's cultural capital.

We hope that this guide has provided you with the inspiration and practical information needed to make your Kyoto adventure truly unforgettable. May your journey be filled with wonder, beauty, and self-discovery as you explore the best that Kyoto has to offer.

Printed in Great Britain
by Amazon

34224027R00098